Saxophone

INTRODUCTION

Welcome back to FastTrack®!

Hope you enjoyed *Saxophone 1* and are ready to play some hits. Have you and your friends formed a band? Or do you feel like soloing with the audio? Either way, make sure you're relaxed and your fingers limber...it's time to play!

With the knowledge you already have from *Saxophone 1*, you're ready to play all eight of these great songs. But it's still important to remember the three Ps: **patience**, **practice** and **pace yourself**.

As with *Saxophone 1*, don't try to bite off more than you can chew. If your lips tire, take some time off. If you get frustrated, put down your sax and just listen to the audio. If you forget something, go back to the method book and learn it. If you're doing fine, think about booking time at a local recording studio!

CONTENTS

ABOUT THE AUDIO

Again, you get audio with the book! Each song in the book is included, so you can hear how it sounds and play along when you're ready.

Each audio example is preceded by one measure of "clicks" to indicate the tempo and meter. Pan right to hear the saxophone part emphasized. Pan left to hear the accompaniment (the band) emphasized.

PLAYBACK+
Speed • Pitch • Balance • Loop

To access audio visit:
www.halleonard.com/mylibrary

Enter Code
7322-1513-2085-6648

ISBN 978-0-634-00982-2

HAL•LEONARD®

Visit Hal Leonard Online at
www.halleonard.com

Contact us:
Hal Leonard
7777 West Bluemound Road
Milwaukee, WI 53213
Email: info@halleonard.com

In Europe, contact:
Hal Leonard Europe Limited
42 Wigmore Street
Marylebone, London, W1U 2RN
Email: info@halleonardeurope.com

In Australia, contact:
Hal Leonard Australia Pty. Ltd.
4 Lentara Court
Cheltenham, Victoria, 3192 Australia
Email: info@halleonard.com.au

LEARN SOMETHING NEW EACH DAY

We know you're eager to play, but first you need to learn a few new things. We'll make it brief—only two pages...

What? Two Staves?!

Don't panic—the top staff is the vocal line, including the lyrics. Most of the time, you'll be playing the same melody, but when you aren't this top staff will help you know where you are in the song.

Oh yeah, "Silhouette" has only one staff. Why? It's a sax solo!

Keys

You'll also quickly notice that your part and the vocal part are in completely different keys. No, this isn't some sort of experimental modern notation. Remember from the end of *Saxophone 1* that your part is always **transposed**.

Endings

Several of the songs have some interesting little symbols that you must understand before playing. Each of these symbols represents a different type of **ending**.

1st, 2nd and 3rd Endings

These are indicated by brackets and numbers.

Simply play the song through to the first ending, then repeat back to the first repeat sign, or beginning of the song (whichever is the case). Play through the song again, but skip the first ending and play the second ending.

One song, "Jailhouse Rock," has a **3rd ending**. But this is really the same principle as a 2nd ending—just one more repeat and ending for one more terrific melody.

D.S. al Coda

When you see these words, go back and repeat from this symbol: 𝄋

Play until you see the words "To Coda," then skip to the Coda, indicated by this symbol: 𝄌

Now just finish the song.

What Is That Little Symbol?

That little dot/moon over the rest at the end of several songs is called a **fermata**.

It simply means to "hold" an unspecified amount of time. That is to say that the tempo will not be the same during a fermata. You can hold the note (or rest) as long as you like. (Of course, we didn't want to keep paying the band, so we just cut them off after a few beats.)

Song Structure

Most songs have different sections, which might be recognizable by any or all of the following:

 INTRODUCTION (or "intro"): This is a short section at the beginning that (you guessed it again!) "introduces" the song to the listeners.

 VERSES: One of the main sections of the song is the **verse**. There will usually be several verses, all with the same music but each with different lyrics.

 CHORUS: Perhaps the most memorable section of a song is the **chorus**. Again, there might be several choruses, but each chorus will often have the same lyrics and music.

 BRIDGE: This section makes a transition from one part of a song to the next. For example, you may find a **bridge** between the chorus and next verse.

 SOLOS: Sometimes **solos** are played over the verse or chorus structure, but in some songs the solo section has its own structure. This is your time to shine!

 OUTRO: Similar to the "intro," this section brings the song to an end.

That's about it! Enjoy the music...

Evil Ways

Words and Music by Sonny Henry

Intro

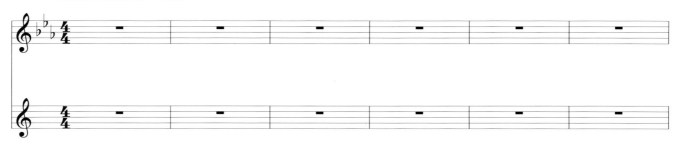

1. You got to change your e – vil ways, ba –

– by, be – fore I start lov – in' you. You got to

change, ___ ba – by, and ev – 'ry word ___ that I

say is true. You got me run-nin' and hid-in' all _____ o - ver town. You got me

sneak-in' and peep-in' and run-nin' me down. This can't go on. Lord knows you got to

change, ba - by, ba - by, 2. When I come

Verse

home, ba - by, my house is dark and my

thoughts are cold. You hang a - round, _____ ba - by,

with Gene and Joan, and a who knows who. I'm get-tin' tired of wait-in' and

fool-in' a - round. I'll find some-bod-y that won't make me feel like a clown. This can't go on.

Solo

Lord knows you got to change.

Verse

3. When I come home, ba-

-by, my house is dark and my thoughts are cold. You hang a-

round, __ ba — by, with Gene and Joan __ and a

who knows who. I'm get - tin' tired ___ of wait - in' and fool - in' a - round. ___ I'll find some -

bod - y that won't make me feel like a clown. This can't go on. Yeah, yeah, yeah. ___

Hey, hey.

Outro

I Want to Hold Your Hand

Words and Music by John Lennon and Paul McCartney

Intro
Moderately ♩ = 136

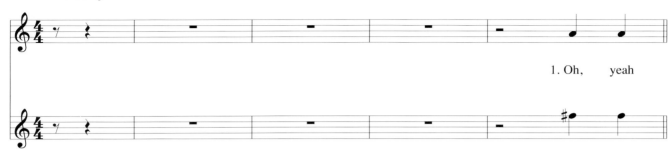

1. Oh, yeah

Verse

I'll _____ tell you some - thing I think you'll un - der - stand. When

I _____ say that some - thing, I want to hold your hand. _____

Chorus

I want to hold your hand _____ I want to hold your _____

Verse

hand.　　　2. Oh,　please ＿＿ say to me ＿＿　　you'll let me be your
　　　　　　　you ＿＿　　got that some - thing　　I think you'll un - der

man.　　　And　please ＿＿ say to me ＿＿　　you'll let me hold your hand. ＿
stand.　　When I ＿＿　　say that some - thing　　I want to hold your hand. ＿

Chorus

＿＿　　Now let me hold your　hand ＿＿＿＿＿＿　　I want to hold　your ＿
＿＿　　I want to hold your　hand ＿＿＿＿＿＿　　I want to hold　your ＿

Bridge

hand. ⎱
hand. ⎰　　　And when I touch you I feel hap - py　in -

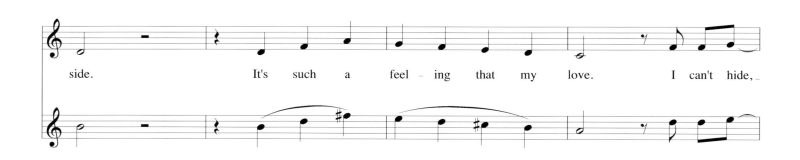

side.　　　It's such a feel - ing that my love.　I can't hide, ＿

I can't hide, ____ I can't hide. ____

3. Yeah,
4. Yeah,

Verse

you ____ got that some - thing I think you'll un - der - stand. When

I ____ feel that some - thing I want to hold your hand. ____

Outro - Chorus

I want to hold your hand, ____ I want to hold your

hand, I want to hold your hand.

gliss.

◆3 In the Mood

By Joe Garland

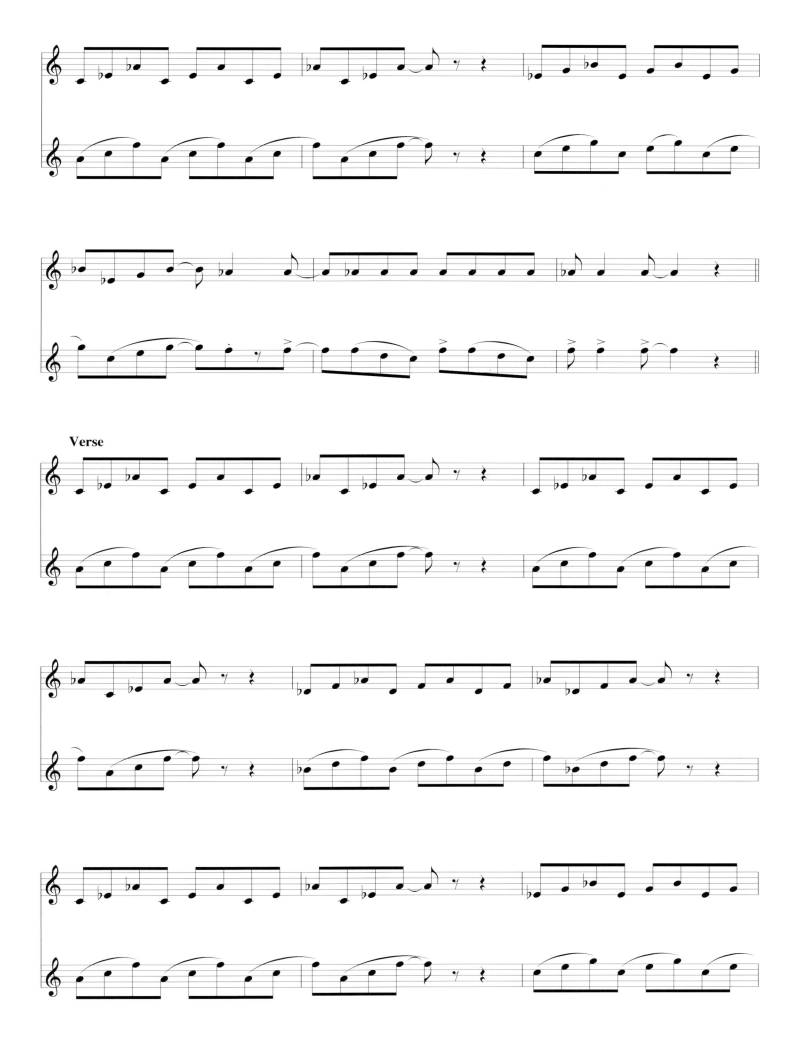

Verse

Chorus

Chorus

Jailhouse Rock

Words and Music by Jerry Leiber and Mike Stoller

Intro

Fast Rock 'n' Roll ♩ = 165

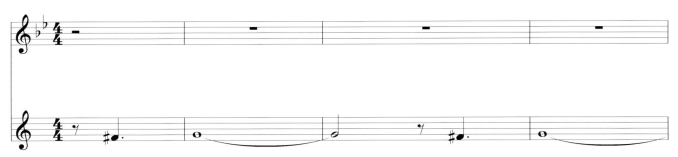

Verse

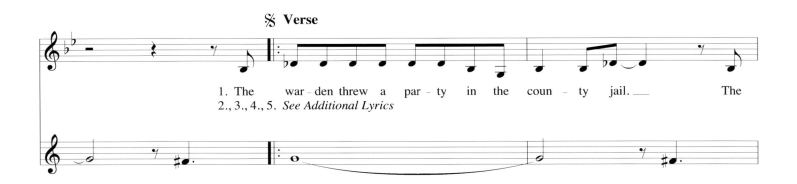

1. The war – den threw a par – ty in the coun – ty jail. ___ The
2., 3., 4., 5. *See Additional Lyrics*

pri – son band was there, and they be – gan to wail. The band was jump-in' and the joint be –

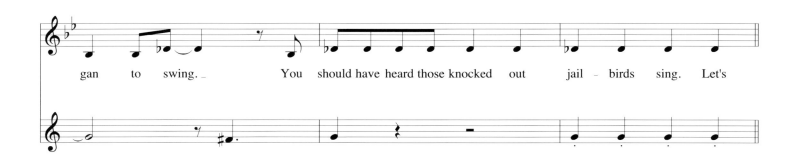

gan to swing. ___ You should have heard those knocked out jail – birds sing. Let's

⊕ Coda

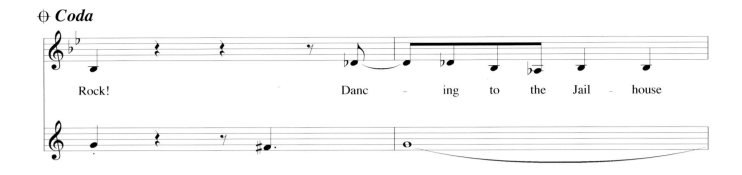

Rock!   Danc - ing to the Jail - house

Rock!   Danc - ing to the Jail - house Rock!

Additional Lyrics

2. Spider Murphy played the tenor saxophone.
   Little Joe was blowin' on the slide trombone.
   The drummer boy from Illinois went crash boom bang.
   The whole rhythm section was the purple gang.

3. Number Forty-seven said to number Three:
   "You're the cutest jailbird I ever did see.
   I sure would be delighted with your company.
   Come on and do the Jailhouse Rock with me."

4. The sad sack was a-sittin' on a block of stone.
   Way over in a corner weeping all alone.
   The warden said, "Hey, Buddy, don't you be no square,
   If you can't find a partner, use a wooden chair."

(optional)

5. Shifty Henry said to Bugs, "For heaven's sake.
   No one's lookin', now's our chance to make a break."
   Bugsy turned to Shifty and he said, "Nix, nix;
   I wanna stick around a while and get my kicks."

Oh, Pretty Woman

Words and Music by Roy Orbison and Bill Dees

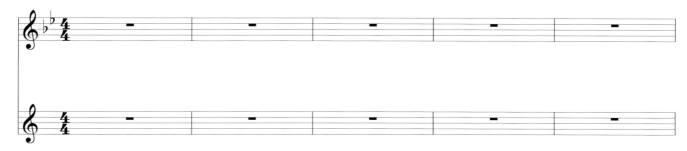

Intro

Moderate Rock ♩ = 130

1. Pret - ty

% Verse

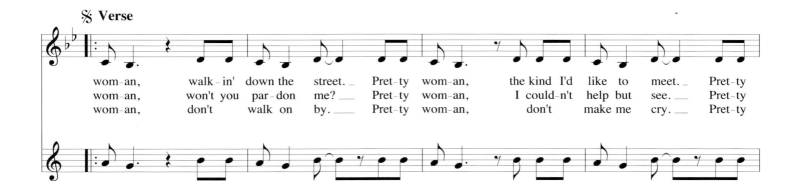

wom – an,　walk - in' down the　street.＿ Pret - ty wom - an,　the kind I'd　like to　meet.＿ Pret - ty

wom – an,　won't you par - don　me?＿ Pret - ty wom - an,　I could-n't　help but　see.＿ Pret - ty

wom – an,　don't　walk on　by.＿ Pret - ty wom - an,　don't　make me　cry.＿ Pret - ty

To Coda ⊕

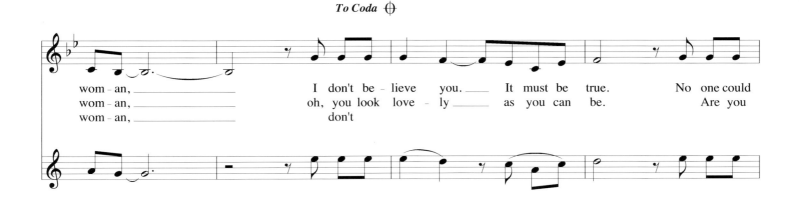

wom – an, ＿＿＿＿＿＿＿　I don't be - lieve　you.＿ It must be　true.　No one could

wom – an, ＿＿＿＿＿＿＿　oh, you look love - ly ＿＿　as you can　be.　Are you

wom – an, ＿＿＿＿＿＿＿　don't

look   as   good   as   you.
lone – ly   just   like   me?

1.   **2.**   **Bridge**

2. Pret – ty   Pret – ty wom – an,

stop   a   while.   Pret – ty wom – an,   talk   a   while.   Pret – ty wom – an,

give   your   smile   to   me.   Pret – ty   wom – an,

yeah, yeah,   yeah.   Pret – ty wom – an   look   my   way.   Pret – ty wom – an

Outro

_k._   I guess I'll go on home. It's late.   There'll be to-

mor - row night, but wait!   What do I see?

Is she walk - ing back to

me?   She's walk - ing back to me.

Whoa,   whoa,   pret - ty wom - an.

Silhouette

By Kenny G

7 Wonderful Tonight

Words and Music by Eric Clapton

Intro
Moderately Slow ♩ = 95

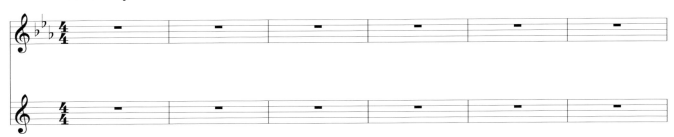

Verse

1. It's late in the eve - 'ning, ___
2. We go to a par - ty, ___
3. It's time to go home ___ now.

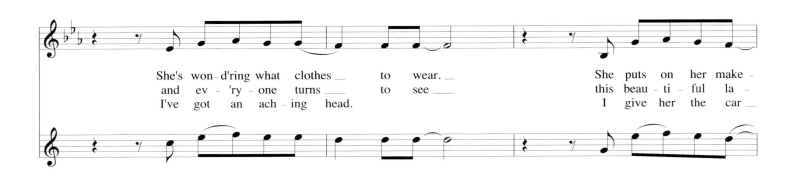

She's won - d'ring what clothes ___ to wear. ___   She puts on her make -
and ev - 'ry - one turns ___ to see ___   this beau - ti - ful la -
I've got an ach - ing head.   I give her the car ___

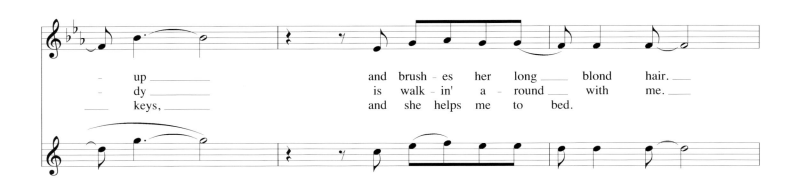

- up   and brush - es her long ___ blond hair. ___
- dy ___   is walk - in' a - round ___ with me. ___
- keys, ___   and she helps me to bed.

To Coda

And then she askes ___ me, ___ "Do I look al – right?" ___
And then she asks ___ me, ___ "Do ya feel al – right?" ___
And then I tell ___ her, ___ as I turn out the light, ___

And I say, "Yes, ___ you look won – der – ful ___ to – night." ___
And I say, "Yes, ___ I feel won – der – ful ___ to – night." ___
I say, "My darlin', ___ you are won – der – ful ___ to – night." ___

1.

2.

Bridge

I feel won – der – ful ___ be – cause I see ___ the love ___

light in ___ your eyes. ___ And the won – der of it all ___

is that you just don't __ re - al - ize __ how much __ I love __

__ you.

D.S. al Coda

Ø *Coda*

Oh, my dar - lin', you are won - der - ful __ to - night. __

Outro

Your Song

Words and Music by Elton John and Bernie Taupin

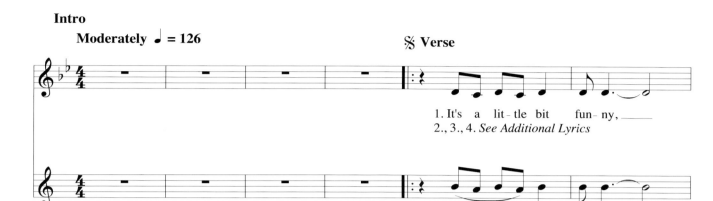

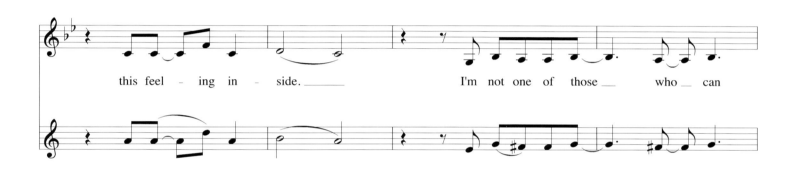

Chorus

And you — can tell ev - 'ry - bod — y this — is your song. —

It may — be quite — sim - ple, but now that it's done, —

I hope you don't mind, I hope you don't mind that I put down in words —

— how won - der - ful life is — while you're — in — the world. —

To Coda ⊕

⊕ **Coda**

I hope you don't mind,   I hope you don't mind   that I put ___ down in

words _____ how won – der – ful life is ___ while

Outro

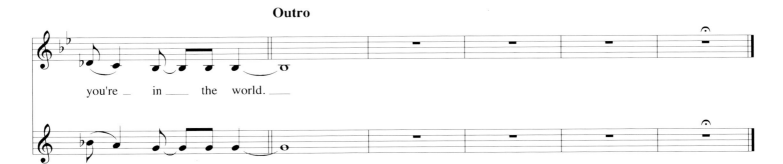

you're _ in ___ the world. ___

Additional Lyrics

2. If I was a sculptor, but then again no
   or a man who makes potions in a travelin' show...
   I know it's not much, but it's the best I can do.
   My gift is my song and this one's for you.

3. I sat on the roof and kicked off the moss.
   Well, a few of the verses well, they've got me quite cross.
   But the sun's been quite kind while I wrote this song.
   It's for people like you that keep it turned on.

4. So excuse me forgetting, but these things I do.
   You see I've forgotten if they're green, ha, or they're blue.
   Anyway, the thing is, what I really mean,
   Yours are the sweetest eyes I've ever seen.

FastTrack is the fastest way for beginners to learn to play the instrument they just bought. **FastTrack** is different from other method books: we've made our book/audio packs user-friendly with plenty of cool songs that make it easy and fun for players to teach themselves. Plus, the last section of the **FastTrack** books have the same songs so that students can form a band and jam together. Songbooks for Guitar, Bass, Keyboard and Drums are all compatible, and feature eight songs including hits such as Wild Thing • Twist and Shout • Layla • Born to Be Wild • and more! All packs include great play-along audio with a professional-sounding back-up band.

FASTTRACK GUITAR

For Electric or Acoustic Guitar – or both!
by Blake Neely & Jeff Schroedl
Book/Audio Packs

Teaches music notation, tablature, full chords and power chords, riffs, licks, scales, and rock and blues styles. Method Book 1 includes 73 songs and examples.

LEVEL 1
00697282	Method Book	$7.99
00697287	Songbook 1	$12.95
00695343	Songbook 2	$12.99
00696438	Rock Songbook 1	$12.99
00696057	DVD	$7.99

LEVEL 2
00697286	Method Book	$9.99
00697296	Songbook 1	$12.95
00695344	Songbook 2	$12.95

CHORDS & SCALES
00697291	9" x 12"	$10.99
00696588	Spanish Edition	$9.99

FASTTRACK BASS

by Blake Neely & Jeff Schroedl
Book/Audio Packs

Everything you need to know about playing the bass, including music notation, tablature, riffs, licks, scales, syncopation, and rock and blues styles. Method Book 1 includes 75 songs and examples.

LEVEL 1
00697284	Method Book	$7.99
00697289	Songbook 1	$12.95
00695368	Songbook 2	$12.95
00696440	Rock Songbook 1	$12.99
00696058	DVD	$7.99

LEVEL 2
00697294	Method Book	$9.99
00697298	Songbook 1	$12.99
00695369	Songbook 2	$12.95

FASTTRACK KEYBOARD

For Electric Keyboard, Synthesizer, or Piano
by Blake Neely & Gary Meisner
Book/Audio Packs

Learn how to play that piano today! With this book you'll learn music notation, chords, riffs, licks, scales, syncopation, and rock and blues styles. Method Book 1 includes over 87 songs and examples.

LEVEL 1
00697283	Method Book	$7.99
00697288	Songbook 1	$12.95
00695366	Songbook 2	$12.95
00696439	Rock Songbook 1	$12.99
00696060	DVD	$7.99
00695594	Spanish Edition	$7.99

LEVEL 2
00697293	Method Book	$9.95
00697297	Songbook 1	$12.95

CHORDS & SCALES
00697292	9" x 12"	$9.99

FASTTRACK DRUM

by Blake Neely & Rick Mattingly
Book/Audio Packs

With this book, you'll learn music notation, riffs and licks, syncopation, rock, blues and funk styles, and improvisation. Method Book 1 includes over 75 songs and examples.

LEVEL 1
00697285	Method Book	$7.99
00697290	Songbook 1	$12.99
00695367	Songbook 2	$12.95
00696441	Rock Songbook 1	$12.99

LEVEL 2
00697295	Method Book	$9.99
00697299	Songbook 1	$12.95
00695371	Songbook 2	$12.95
00696059	DVD	$7.99

FASTTRACK SAXOPHONE

by Blake Neely
Book/Audio Packs

With this book, you'll learn music notation; riffs, scales, keys; syncopation; rock and blues styles; and more. Includes 72 songs and examples.

LEVEL 1
00695241	Method Book	$7.95
00695409	Songbook	$12.95
00696657	Spanish Edition	$7.99

FASTTRACK HARMONICA

by Blake Neely & Doug Downing
Book/Audio Packs

These books cover all you need to learn C Diatonic harmonica, including: music notation • singles notes and chords • riffs, licks & scales • syncopation • rock and blues styles. Method Book 1 includes over 70 songs and examples.

LEVEL 1
00695407	Method Book	$7.99
00695574	Songbook	$12.99

LEVEL 2
00695889	Method Book	$9.95
00695891	Songbook	$12.99

FASTTRACK LEAD SINGER

by Blake Neely
Book/Audio Packs

Everything you need to be a great singer, including: how to read music, microphone tips, warm-up exercises, ear training, syncopation, and more. Method Book 1 includes 80 songs and examples.

LEVEL 1
00695408	Method Book	$7.99
00695410	Songbook	$12.95
00696589	Spanish Edition	$7.99

LEVEL 2
00695890	Method Book	$9.95
00695892	Songbook 1	$12.95

Visit Hal Leonard online at **www.halleonard.com**